# Love's "Vertical" Address

By Devin T. Robinson X "Egypt"

She gave up fighting.
Being a "good girl" was not enough
She gave up fighting

He wanted more
Decided sex would open the door
He wanted more

She spread her legs
Hoping to find love
She spread her legs

He invited her in
She obliged.
He invited her in

She discovered a secret
Love never entered the bed sheets

She discovered a secret

He climaxed and whispered… "I love you"
She heard him…but replied, "Thank you"
He climaxed and whispered… "I love you"
She heard him…but replied, "I heard you the first time"

She waited for him to say, "I love you"
He never did…
She said, "Baby…I love you"
He said, " I love me too"
She waited for him to say, "I love you"
He left without an utterance

Heart broken she was
Broken hearted he was
Both donated their bodies in search of love
Both only finding pain and regret
Where is the treasure map for love?
What is the address for your GPS?

If it's not heaven…you are misdirected.

Two different stories
Of four different people
In two different cities
In two different states.
With the same outcome…
They all realized…sadly
Love Is Not An STD

# Chapter 1:

# Love suffers...

Who do you love? What did they do for your love? Here is the most provocative question, what did they endure for your love?

Drunken love without endurance is bound to become sober self-hate. Why? Who do we eventually blame for our broken hearts? After a while, the fingers point at ourselves for allowing someone something so beautiful without ever suffering through anything or earning such a blessing.

A mother doesn't love her baby solely because the child is hers. She loves because for 9 months she suffered swollen feet, odd hormonal transitions and a beach ball belly. She went through something for this miracle.

You love your parents because of what they endured to have you. Not just the pregnancy and labor but financial struggles, your mistakes…etc. If this is untrue, why don't you love a stranger the same as your father or mother?

Our society neglects the idea of "endurance" for love. Thus is why we have quick loves, fast marriages and even faster divorces. Most arrangements are based off lust, infatuation, greed or the desire to isolate that person from another suitor. Is this the love you want?

1st Corinthians 13: 4-8 is a famous passage in the Holy Bible about love. Can you say your love matches it? Do you donate love in the same manner? Are you being loved the same?

# Chapter 2:

## Do you F.I.S.L.E ®?

Many relationships don't "F.I.S.L.E" because we miss out on true displays of affection. Not sexual, physical or monetary, but those things you can't put a price on. Do you F.I.S.L.E ®?

Faith, Inspiration, Support, Leadership and Education (F.I.S.L.E) ® is a theory I use to advise my clients on self-worth and "earnership". If the person can give you all five, then they are giving you something truly remarkable and worthwhile…they are…earning you and eventually your love. Hopefully you are reciprocating otherwise its like cooking steak…with no heat…or oven…or steak.

# Faith

Is this person helping to cultivate your love with God? Are you praying, reading, researching, studying and serving together? Also, if your response to, "Do you pray together?" falls under the following replies, "We used to.", "Occasionally" or "No" then how can you love if you don't talk to the One who created the word?

If God is love and you are not growing in God, how can you grow in love?

# Inspiration

A great coach inspires their players. Relationships are like basketball games. If you are not inspired, you won't produce the best. If your mate is not encouraging you to be the best you, then forget about the playoffs. Even if you make it to the finals, you can win and enjoy the championship day. However, it will be short lived because without inspiration...you won't repeat the championship.

# Support

How would a pastor feel if he walked into an empty church 52 Sundays a year? Sure, he could give a dynamic speech, deliver a sermon that would save the most "unsavable" souls but...if no one ever attended...would he have the fire to keep it up year after year? We would hope so but sometimes hope is a drug for fools.

In reality, he would regroup and research tactics to create a congregation to give the word of God.

Many toxic relationships involve one or two parties whom are not supporting each other's dreams, hopes or aspirations. She wants to dance but he won't attend a practice, watch her perform or assist in any capacity. He wants to box but she has never visited the gym, massaged his aching muscles or run a hot bath for him. Without support, love is like a ship in…the desert.

# Leadership

Crack leads some people to kill, steal and hurt even those they love. No…it's the choice to be led by crack …not the crack. When we choose to lead a relationship in the right direction, it will go there. If we don't choose…then it's based on foolish hope that we will reach where we want to go.

Our poisonous relationships of today don't involve leadership. More so a, "Hope we make it"-ship. Did you sit down and say, "This is where I want to go…can you lead me?" If you have not, why indulge in anger when you don't reach your desired destination?

If you jumped in a taxi but never told him where to take you, yet he began to drive and you ended up at a strip club instead of church…who is at fault? The taxi driver for leading without direction, you for not asking "Can you take me to church?" or you both for not discussing "Where are we headed"?

Pray about choosing someone who can lead and being a leader. Both parties must lead in different areas to arrive on time.

When you have a road trip, you may not ride the entire way by yourself because when you're tired, you give the wheel to someone you trust to guide you safely to the desired location.... right? It works the same in the relationship. If you have to question, "Can they lead me?" or " Can I lead them?" then...there is a diabolical meltdown on the rise...wait and see.

When two people come together to lead, they're leading towards the SAME goal. There is no guessing or allowing chance to be part of this equation.

If I ask a woman, "Where are you to heading in your relationship?" if her response is, "I don't know. We're just taking it as it comes" to me I've heard more than she said.

What she really said was, "I'm being led by a man who isn't leading me anywhere. I've probably asked but he's giving no direction. Therefore, instead of rocking the "boat to nowhere", I rather stay on the "cruise of confusion."

No one-person leads a relationship, they both co-lead. We all have different strengths. We all have something unique to offer. We all MUST head in the same direction otherwise you aren't going anywhere. As a matter of fact, you will no longer be permitted to call your union a relationship but a relationSTOP."

## Education

A man or woman who can't educate you is much like a man or woman who thinks they know too much to be educated… a waste, future stress and an eventual ex. What would we be without education?

First…reading this would be impossible. Secondly, there would not be any growth. When you are dating someone who can teach you about God, life, geography, music, animals, life experiences, food, vacation spots, finances, real estate…etc. you grow something that can't be replaced or disvalued.

Many people I advise can't tell me one thing their mate has taught them. Nor can they inform me of something they educationally infected them with. You don't come into a relationship to stay the way you were, but to become something new. If you are walking with God but are the same person you were before you took the first step…you never started walking.

# Chapter 3:
# Missing Elements of Love

Here's a magic trick.

    I want you to blow up a balloon using only your breath.
After you've filled the bubble, I want you to tie the ends.
Lastly, release and allow it to fly.
The goal is for the balloon to reach the ceiling on its own.
Now, go make magic!
Take your time. I'll wait....

As you're probably realizing...the balloon isn't rising.
Even if you attempt to do it again...the balloon won't rise.

Maybe your breath isn't special.
Or…you just tied it too tight?
Wait…I know…you bought the wrong balloon.

I trust you figured out what you are missing.
Helium.
Without helium, the balloon won't ascend.

Where am I going?

    Our love falls, just like the balloon. We try and try and try to make it work. Consistently placing the wrong element into the balloon, such as more trust, more sex and more blind faith. Yet, it still doesn't work. What is the reasoning behind this?

    Most "Loving" relationships fail because they're missing vital elements. We say "I love you" but what is involved inside those three historic words? We fall in love with people who have simply not proven they CAN love us.

What happens after you say, "I love you"? You begin to permit "chances." Have you noticed we do some of the craziest things while in love? That's because love gives us an excuse to accept the flaws, mistakes and horribly selfish decision making of others. Now, just imagine if you say, "I love you" to someone who didn't first make you F.I.S.L.E? What happens if you say, "I love you" to someone who didn't earn you? What happens if you say, "I love you" to someone but there was a missing element to your love? What would happen? You two will do things you normally don't do, wouldn't allow or never imagined…for someone who won't be there tomorrow.

Once you F.I.S.LE, odds are you will fall in love. There are many books written about love however, in order to truly give reason as to understand love, there are three elements many don't own inside their love:

- Time
- Endurance
- Trust

## Time:

How long have you known this person to truly say, "I love" them?
The average is 88 days for men and 134 days for women according to a national survey by Dailymail.com. I say 12 months minimum. As I've used in previous relationships.

My current relationship timeline goes as followed: We met January 2011. Became exclusive (Boyfriend and Girlfriend) and exchanged, " I love you" on August 2012. August 2013 we were engaged and (God willing) April 6th 2014 we'll be married.

Altogether this journey totals about 40 months of knowing each other, 18 months TO love each other, 12 months OF loving each other before we decided to love each other…for the rest of our lives. It may seem long to you or may not. Whatever it appears, this is much more successful than ANY other relationship I rushed into in my past 4 attempts. All ended in breakups and the last two didn't build my esteem but all were, "Loved".

Out of 5 girlfriends (as an adult…can't count middle school…I was calling any girl my girlfriend) only 1 led to marriage. That means my ratio is 1 out of 5, a measly 20% success rate. Think about yours. Take the person you're married to or about to marry and divide them against all the people you dated after you turned 18. ***Ex: 1/5=20***. That's your success rate. I'm 20%. (Which is much lower than the average divorce rate of 50%. I'm winning!)

Now, if none of your relationships ended in marriage, your current success rate is 0%. Therefore, if you've been falling in love quick or believing any of the above to be false, you hopefully have an algorithm to follow which proves why time is important. (Wife or Husband Divided By Failed Relationships=Relational Success Rate.) Remember, if that first number is 0 then the last number is 0 too. Time doesn't mean the person will marry you but at least with time… you'll know if they're worth marrying.

When you watch a movie or TV show have you noticed the average time people fall in love is two weeks to a month?

To the reader, this may seem, "sane", as you're supposed to think. Technology has increased our ability to communicate, invade the lives of others and expose our flaws or personal thoughts without a veil of privacy. This means something truly tragic.

We love people too soon to love, understand and accept their imperfections. We're just forced to accept people we know too much about under the idea of "we know them." In reality, we don't know them. We know about them, we know what they tell us but…is such enough to "love" someone? What did you really learn about them to solicit "love" as a valid title to express the feeling you own?

Honestly, when I ask clients, "Why do you love them?" most of the time the response is, "I've been with them for so long…etc" They fell in love way before, "so long." It's a guise we use to explain falling in love with someone's attention, time and our desire to be loved. That's actually what we fall in love with. Attention, seemingly exclusive time and the desire to be loved with an occasional drop of circumstance.

Have you noticed we typically fall in love faster when we're broken? When leaving a bad relationship, we tend to have a "Heal me" mentality. It's mostly subconscious since during such time many say, "I'm NEVER dating again" yet we fall, fall fast and fall hard. Why?

The desire to be loved outweighs our desire to be loved right. Which amplifies the moments we share with the person. Everything they say is more potent. (Especially if it's the right thing we wanted to hear) Time seems to fly while we await their calls, touch or visit. Sadly, that's just infatuation covered in desperation. How can we say, "I love you" to someone we haven't known long enough to even honestly say, "I love you" to?

Infatuation comes early, fast and heavy. After it wanes, we are kept by the contempt of our traditional bond with "love." Meaning we won't leave even though we should simply because, "Love is supposed to be a forever commitment." If not that, we stay solely because we've invested so much time into that person, we don't want another to enjoy them or endure life alone.

Why does infatuation fade? The representative dies courtesy of their realization that they "have" you. Which means, now that there is nothing they can get from you, there is no other reason to treat you the way you deserve. They go on, "autopilot." No longer aiming to please you, just creating a "just enough" atmosphere to keep you entertained or themselves entertained until the end comes. Don't believe me?

Have you ever heard or been told. "You aren't the same person anymore"? How about, "You've changed"? or "You stopped doing the things I fell in love with"? Odds are…yes. That's either from relationship fatigue (The result of being in a dead-end relationship for too long.) or being with someone you didn't know in the first place.

That person didn't have enough time to show you their true colors. You just took the representative given, applied, "Love" to it and now you're stuck with someone who isn't who they were but who they are and that "who" isn't the "who" you fell in love with.

What would happen if you took time to know the person you would eventually love?

What would happen if you said, "I won't love someone until they've been with me for at least 6-12 months"?

What would happen if you didn't love someone just because of how they treated you but how they treated everyone around them, their parents, their community, their future and themselves for an extended period of time?

Take your time to say, "I love you." Why? When you say those words, you write a contract on your heart. You agree to never give up on love. You make a promise to give them chances that unearned love earned them.

Q. Why do you think some women stay after the first punch?
A. *Love.*
Q. Why do some men allow women to play them consistently?
A. *Love.*
Q. Why do some people make babies just to keep a person there?
A. *Love.*

Be careful. Take your time. 3-6 months isn't long enough.
How could you REALLY know someone in that time?
If I'm wrong, how many of your relationships ended in marriage?

Think about it. We've been fooled by a society of people who fall in love quick and divorce even quicker.

Time. Use it. Such helps with the next element...

## Endurance:

Want to know why most good people date bad people?
Bad people offer drama that good people avoid. Good people tend to detour their lives away from drama...bad people drive towards or create it.

Drama is exciting! All great stories have some form of drama but there is a difference between drama and endurance. Drama is self-inflicted. Something you do that caused a chain of undesirable events to occur. Endurance is something you react to. A chain of unexpected events you handle to achieve a desirable goal.

The Holy Bible is a great tool to find both.

***Example:*** The story of David and Goliath! David volunteered to fight a giant! This was to the death! What weapon did he have? Gun? Cannon? Tank? No...a sling and rocks. Was David massive? No. Yet with a small frame, tiny weapon but HUGE faith in God...David killed Goliath (Sorry to spoil the ending for you). He didn't become just famous giant killer, but a KING! That wasn't the dramatic part of his story. The dramatic part was when King David sent a woman's husband to the front lines of an army so the husband would die and King David could have the dead husband's wife. King David lost favor with God because of his actions.

Drama "is self-inflicted. Something you do that caused a chain of undesirable events to occur." David didn't have to have a man killed for another wife. He was a king. There were many other women. Why lose favor courtesy of selfish desire? He was still elevated by God but imagine how David's story would have been minus the drama?

Endurance was David reacting to Goliath's cursing, tempting and taunting. His people were in fear. They needed hope. Therefore, David became that hope amongst the fearful to bring about peace and victory. David probably didn't expect everyone to avoid challenging Goliath. No matter the fact, he had to achieve his goal. Remember, endurance: "A chain of unexpected events you handle to achieve a desirable goal."

Bad boys and girls are known for drama. Either they have children they don't take care of or care for, jobs they aren't good at or don't have or excuses they own...but never rent. Whatever the reasoning, there is always an issue with them. Funny thing, it's always someone else's fault. Yet, when you dig deep...their disposition is a result of an action THEY did. They are COMPLETELY at blame for the equation ending as so. Amazingly, that doesn't keep good men and women from entertaining them. Why? Drama is addictively attractive!

Drama, to responsible adults, is intriguing. Any responsible person can't honestly understand the thinking of an irresponsible person. It's quite a site to see for them. When you're an adult, watching someone your age act as if the world owes him or her something is primetime TV. It's comparable to watching a top movie...you didn't pay for. This is the beauty behind their ugly immaturity. It's entertainment at its finest. The only problem is when you stop watching the show and become a supporting character.

## Short _TRUE_ Story.

I dated a lesbian (Yes...I thought the same as well) for about three months. Inside these three months, I lost a PATCH of hair dealing with her seemingly daily demonic desire to argue. At a time, we actually argued about not arguing. Yes...a sad time in my life. Yet, why did I stay with her for three months? It was the drama. She was lost in her future, sexuality and purpose. A dead end job, fluctuating impression of women and a new man who made her like men again. Each day was another reason for her to go half-crazy. Every argument was just her lashing out at the horrible decisions she made successfully. I was her verbal punching bag. She kept breaking pieces of my spirit and I couldn't figure out how to leave until I reached what I tell my clients, "a catastrophe moment."

That's when the drama hits an unexpected peak and you find yourself unable to go any further. It's comparable to learning your mate has a child from someone else, isn't planning on leaving the person they slept with and wants you to stay to "be part of the family." You might hit a boiling point and say, "I'm done." That's the "catastrophe moment."

Endurance is what good people offer. You'll note, most good people have healthy things to endure. Tough class before graduation, career searches after a recession and loan dept they are actively paying off. When unexpected events occur, they handle them the best they could. It's not them that caused it, but they take care of it. Why? That's what adults do. Many relationships are filled with drama and when the drama hits the "catastrophe moment" they give up. Only if they had to endure life...they would find more than enough to endure.

Life has its own version of drama called..."life." There is nothing you can do to avoid it and you must deal with it. Trust me from finding yourself, landing a career, understanding your new boss, meeting the love of your life, communicating properly with them, wedding planning, marriage, moving in together, dealing with in-laws, pregnancy, a child, potty training, pre-school, sending a child off to college, paying for their marriage...etc, there is MUCH to do. It's unavoidable but something responsible people do. Sometimes responsible people make mistakes and have to deal with drama. They aren't immune to its glamour. Typically their mistake is dating someone who is drama prone. In the end, life is enough for any and everyone.

When it comes to love, endurance is what strengthens it. Going through life together with someone who will fight with you, not give you more things to fight. That's what endurance does. It builds. Like muscles.

Once you've done 10 push ups a day for a week, the next week you can do 11. Why? You constructed muscle either mentally or physically and endured enough to reach another plateau. The drama version would be trying to do a push up but because your priorities are a mess, you never get a chance to. What is the end result? One person is built up on a foundation of the "Obstacle +Effort = Success" equation. The other added to the "Obstacle + No Effort = More Obstacles" equation.

Love someone who you can endure life with. Avoid being yoked with someone who can only bring drama to your life.

This transitions beautifully to my next element.

## Trust:

In my very popular workshop, "Love Is Not An STD", I'll ask a volunteer to stand in front of me with their eyes closed then fall back and TRUST I will catch them.

Many times the volunteer apprehensively falls back until about the fifth time. Then they fall without worry. Why? I earned their TRUST simply because I caught them four times. Now they TRUST my arms will be there the fifth time. This is how it works.

Trust is a vital component to love. Do you trust the person you love with your soul? It's a real question. Do you trust them with your life? Honestly, ask yourself. Do you trust them with your future? If not, then why love them? This is why time and endurance is needed BEFORE you say, "I love you" and WHILE you're in that love.

We love people we don't trust. If you're worried about them cheating, stealing or lying, then you shouldn't be in love with them. That's not healthy. That's not "natural" that's called, "poisonous." You don't trust them because they consciously or subconsciously gave you a reason to not trust them. If that was after you said, "I love you" then now you're in a heap of trouble. Since now you'll be in denial while you attempt to overshadow your false love with the hopes love will be enough to get you through life. Sorry…love is not enough.

Without trust, it's like trying to swim with no arms or legs. Yes, there are some amazing people who probably can do it…but it's not recommended.

Have you noticed it's hard to forgive some people and love them again after they've disowned your trust? Odds are, they didn't earn it to begin with and now they're trying to earn something while being in debt with the debtor. Let me break it down with basic arithmetic.

If someone earns your trust in the beginning, they start off with 100. Now, if they mess up with your trust, they go down to 50. At this point, they have to work their way back up to 100. What if they never earned it? What if you loved them out of infatuation but never had to endure life with them to see how they dealt with obstacles as an adult? What if they entered the relationship with drama but you ignored it hoping your trust in them would appear out of thin air?

You see, they started at a false 100. In fact, it was a 0. It was given with potential of being proved. (*Potential is a broken woman's poison...email me and I'll tell you why*) Now when they cheat or lie, they're now at 0.

They give flowers, start sweet-talking, toss money...etc to work their way up. They will only get to 50 but your denial or self lying will commit to trusting them like they are 100 but your heart will only give them 50. Now what? You are half in love. Not fully trusting where they are, what they're saying and who they're with. You force yourself to hold back lashing out. You force yourself from saying, "I don't trust you." You force yourself to trust them. What makes you do this? You said, "I love you." You've written a contract with your heart and don't want the embarrassment of leaving them, confusion with the unknowing direction of dating someone new or pain caused courtesy of them dating someone new. So you stay. Hurt. Broken. Ashamed.

This is what happens when you love people who didn't have to prove themselves worthy of your trust. When you see how they've dealt with life, how you two deal with it together and how the future looks between you two solely because with this person, you can believe a future exists since you trust who they are will be who they will always be, then trust will keep your foundation strong. Life will always donates its hurricanes but a house built on the foundation of time, endurance and trust can afford a little rain.

# Chapter 4:
## Soul Signs of love

This may be the most difficult chapter to agree with at the start. Yet, by the time you've finished reading it may expose flaws in your thinking.

The following are typical attributes ALL people who love you have:
- ➢ Jealous
- ➢ Overprotective
- ➢ Nice
- ➢ Insecure
- ➢ Sensitive

I call this, "JONIS" in my workshop, "Love Is Not An STD"

Coincidentally, these five characteristics are also signs we use to ignore those who can love us. Ironically, when we meet someone who doesn't share these tones of character, we actually encourage them to add one or more to their personal structure.

Ex: If someone sends good morning, afternoon and evening messages daily, they can be seen as "too Nice." When a bad person doesn't do it, the comfortable request is, "Why don't you send me good morning messages?"

Wanting good things from bad people is a sign of insanity. You're setting yourself up for failure when you want good things from bad people. Why? Asking a man with no legs to bike around the world with you isn't a wise move. Since it won't produce the fruit you desire, just drama you should avoid. Additionally, you'll head most of the work. Not him. As many women who date bad boys find out…the hard way.

Let's break down **JONIS.**

## Jealous:

ANYONE who cares for you gets jealous.

If you bragged about someone else's parents to your parents, do you think your parent wouldn't have a self-reflective moment to ponder if they're inadequate at parenting? Same as a man who is dating a woman but she spends her time bragging about other men. Even more common, you're dating a woman and talking about the pros of your ex. They deserve the right to wonder if they're fulfilling you. Jealousy isn't a horrible characteristic. God is jealous. "for I, the LORD your God, am a jealous God" (Exodus 20:4-5)." It's only when that jealousy is in moderation, not extreme usage, when it's healthy.

## Overprotective:

Who can love you without some form of overprotection?
Back to your parents, or guardians who are to love you. Would they enjoy the idea of you going away with strangers for a month without any way of contacting you, checking up on you or knowing you're safe? Odds are…no. They would want to know about your safety, whereabouts and if there's anything they can provide for you.

Many may call that "Overprotective" in the negative, but now that I'm 30, having someone to check up on me is a beautiful thing. It means someone actually has a vested interest in my health. I'm not referring to the person who pops up at your job to see why you haven't returned a call 23 minutes ago. I'm referring to the person who calls the police because they haven't heard from you in 23 hours and you aren't where you said you were going to be.

Have you noticed many of the lost or kidnapped people are typically discovered to be missing within a day? A whole day didn't pass before a relative or person who loved them called the police with, "I called but they normally don't take this long to answer. Went to where they said they were and didn't find them." That's care, not stalkerish.

We should want someone to protect us. Especially as men, we have an innate desire to protect. Most women can attest to not calling her man at the usual time and when she does call or he calls the FIRST thing he says is, "Is everything okay?" Why?

As men, in order to protect you, we first have to create a habit for you. A schedule.

Once we create that schedule, we live by it. You're going to call at a certain time, go home at a certain time or work at a certain time. Whenever you change course, our instincts are alerted to you being out of sync. This is common. Again, I'm not referring to the guy or gal who wants to know where you are, who you're with and why you didn't return the text two seconds ago. That's not overprotective, that's extreme.

# <u>N</u><u>ice:</u>

Most people who lend themselves to others by putting another person's desires ahead of themselves are typically the first to hear the collaboration of these INFAMOUS words, "You're too nice."

People who say this are 9/10 broken folk who've been with too many scoundrels to adhere to someone who is doing what good people do…be nice. There is no such thing as "Too Nice." It's only when we receive something we don't believe we deserve do we ready ourselves to fear, avoid or discard it with harsh words.

How could someone really be too nice to you? Does that make sense? My fiancé set up a high reunion for me at her home because I missed my own. She had videos of my best friends, pictures and a slew of memorabilia commemorating that time in my life. (Those braids in high school were something else, ha!) Was that too nice? No. It wasn't. I deserved it. I was appreciative of it. I enjoyed it. Don't you deserve someone going out of their way to make you smile? If you think not, then I hope whatever minimal effort needed to make you grin is all you desire in life. Odds are…that's all you'll receive.

# Insecure:

We all have our insecurities. It's weird when faced with unique relationship challenges, being "insecure" is a weakness. It's actually human to be insecure.

insecure | ˌinsiˈkyoŏr |
adjective
**1** (of a person) not confident or assured; uncertain and anxious:

Wasn't Jesus at one point insecure about His directive? Didn't He question God?
"...My God, My God, why hast Thou forsaken Me?" Matthew 27:45-46

Those of us in the Christian faith or our Jewish or Muslim brothers or sisters wouldn't dare call Jesus, "weak." It's the proof that we all have our insecurities about life, our purpose and relationships. That doesn't mean this vulnerability is of fools, children and the lame. Strong people can be insecure. It's how faith is built.

When there is too much turbulence on a plane, I get insecure about its safety. Then I pray. When the plane overcomes the shaky moment, my faith has made me well. It has built my belief that next time, if I just have faith in He who I pray to, the unsteadiness will meet steadiness. Also, insecurity is a result of an action. It doesn't appear out of thin air. It's a reaction to something.

If you're dating someone and they are insecure about people you hang around, maybe it's courtesy of the negative influence those people have over you. Maybe they're living their lives incorrectly and your mate fears you may follow foot. This isn't an excuse for them to prevent you from having friends. This is a moment for you to understand a river doesn't run without water. Meaning, there is a root reasoning behind their insecurities.

It could be from past relationships or you. Either or, it's a conversation to be had. The existence of insecurities doesn't mean your relationship is unhealthy, per se. It means communication may lack and there are conferences about this moment needed to eradicate the insecurity.

## Sensitive:

Both men and women have been held up emotionally due to the unleashing of these words upon them. "You're too sensitive." This is probably one of the main reasons why men and women hold back emotions or truth. As humans, being sensitive is natural. In this society, being able to voice how you feel is another sign of weakness. That's horrifically false.

Many people, especially women I counsel, would enjoy hearing how their mate feels, their inner most fears, what makes them refrain from completely loving these women. However, if the words, "You're being sensitive" are used when they express something or "Be a man" then you will get what you ask for.

Being a man in this society equals that of a robot. No emotion, nonchalant and hard working without worry of the future. That's a man. Imagine the 45 year old plumber without any care in the world, goes to work everyday, drinks a beer or two when he gets home, rarely sweet talks his wife, never says, "I love you" to anyone and wouldn't cry if a gun was pointed at his head.

That's this society's image of a real man. Sadly, many have found keeping up that façade is impossible. We break down. We cry. We hurt. We want to tell you, "I need help" but are too afraid of hearing how weak we are. From here…we shut down. Give you nothing but the end result of our day. None of the emotional roller coaster we endured. Just the,

"It was a regular day, babe. Throw me a beer, will ya?" Women suffer similarly.

Men constantly derail your desire to converse about your inner most feelings only to denounce you as, "too emotional." This causes the adverse effect of making her become emotional to those who will listen, not judge and add advice. Being sensitive to things that hurt you is normal. Judging, hurting with words and ignoring a person's paint isn't normal.

Being sensitive is what separates us from machines. My Chihuahua, Kemet cries if I leave for too long. If I don't pet him or ignore him, he'll whine. This isn't "too sensitive" but who he is. If I stop him from being that, I hinder him as he is and what he is at his core.

Be sensitive. It's okay.

# Chapter 5:
# BEWARE OF **NSD!**

Amazingly almost everyone has this disease and yet the Center for Disease Control (CDC) has done nothing to find a cure for it. Why is the CDC afraid to tackle this disease that's sweeping households away? Maybe because it's not found in any book...except this one.

NSD= the Negotiable Standard Disease. Many people start off with basic standards. *Someone who is loving, caring, nice, loyal and trustworthy*, right? Then we may add they *need to have a job, future and no drama*, right? Lastly, they should be *attractive, treat me with respect and be respectful*, right? If that mirrors your basic standards, which are all wonderful and not the least bit unrealistic, why do we settle for someone with no job, multiple children they don't take care of and a future that's about as real as a 6.50$ dollar bill? We got infected.

For many of us, we want to Be Loved Right © so bad…we become desperate. What was basic before becomes hard to find…or we stop looking…or call those who fit our basic desires, "Too good to be true" as I say in my third book, "Change Him…In 100 Pages." We have to stop being so used to running away from people who are "too good to be true" and running to people who are "horrible enough to be realistic."

Why do we think it's okay to give away our time to people who don't meet our basic needs? What do we think will come out of this transaction? Love? How long will this charity of love last? Yes, it's charity. You or they were being charitable. If the above are the basic standards and you or they don't meet the requirements, yet were still given "love", that's charity.

You owe it to yourself to know what you desire is yours to have. However, if you jump at the first available or most persistent yet unqualified pursuer, you're denying yourself what you pray for.

How can God fill your cup with water if you already have dirt inside it? Comparatively, how can He give you a good man or woman while you're still dealing with the mess you decided to love?

Do you think He would send a sheep to a wolf? Even if He did send you what you prayed for, you wouldn't even recognize them as something sent from Him. Why? (I love this question) You'll be too burnt, broken and blinded to be healed by someone who can love you. When you do meet them, instead of loving them as your mate, you'll make them your "friend."

The infamous, "friend zone" is where they will live until someone else takes them off your shelf. This is the reality of life. This is a real disease. Whenever you accept less than you're worth, you should think of that as a sickness.

That isn't a Christian way of thinking. I don't even believe Muslims or Jews believe in accepting people who are unequally yoked as well. Why? Let's first breakdown what it means to be, "Unequally yoked."

In the book, "12 Questions To Ask Before You Marry.", they break down what "Unequally yoked" means.

To summarize, when you plow a field with two oxen, both beasts have to be of the same stature, strength and ability so they can plow the field evenly. When one is stronger than the other, the field is plowed unevenly and can destroy the crop. You are the animals, the plow is your relationship and the field is your life.

Don't allow NSD to be the reason why your love life is uneven. You deserve more. Wait for it.

# Chapter 6:

# Love exercises

If you have not shown love, you may not know what is looks like. Thus is why sex…well…lust gets confused for love. Love is a donation in which you don't look for a return. Your main goal is servitude. Making the person happy. The "Thank you", "I appreciate it" or "You made my day" is extra and not needed. The following exercises are important to finishing this book. Once you're completed, email me at Author@LoveIsNotAnSTD.com on how this experience made you feel.

### *Foot Wash:*

Washing someone's feet is an amazing expression of love, servitude and humbleness. Not only are you beneath them but also serving them a way in which most never enjoy. In order to understand this book about love, you have to taste it.

**Requirements:**

2 wash clothes, 1 bottle of water and willing heart.
Wet one washcloth with the bottle of water. Wipe their feet. Dry their feet with the other cloth. Prior to washing, allow them to know you are doing this to practice love.

1st. A Family Member (Seemingly easiest)
2nd. A Friend (Oddly the oddest)
3rd. A Stranger (The actual easiest…you will see why)

## *Random Love with…a Sticky Tab:*

Attached are 5-10 sticky tabs if not,

please use a sheet of paper, tear it in 5 or 10 pieces or improvise. On each you will write, "God Loves You" or any creative message about love you can. Take such and give it to a total stranger. Please, refrain from placing your name or any identifiable information. This is a donation of love. If they never see you again...good. The focus is to go outside yourself to display love and enjoy the beauty of being that expression of God to someone who may have needed it. You never know, this yellow 3x3 tab might save a life...it saved mine.

## *Love Letter:*

Write a physical letter to someone detailing how much and why you love them then mail it. A physical letter holds more weight than an email simply because it takes more time and energy to send. In addition, letters become their memories of your love investments or reminders for you. Emails just become...deleted.

All of these may not be easy to do at first...or ever, however that is love. Love is not always easy but it is a blessing. It is a gift. Sometimes it's hard to buy a TV for your friend on Black Friday but you endure the hassle for their happiness. You are willing to suffer the crowds, endure the agony of haggling and be patient in long lines...for their happiness.

# Chapter 7:
## Love's Farewell

"Love is patient, love is kind. It does not envy, it does not boast, it is not proud. It is not rude, it is not self-seeking, it is not easily angered, it keeps no record of wrongs. Love does not delight in evil but rejoices with the truth. It always protects, always trusts, always hopes, always perseveres."-I Corinthians 13:4-7

Thank you for taking the time to read this book. As the years pass, these words will change. They will take form as you develop. Why? Love changes, grows and is understood differently. The way you love your parents or friends today will alter in 1-10 years. Ex: I loved my sister for taking care of me after my mother died, when I was 12. Now at 30, I adore her courage, understand her sacrifices and praise her tenacity more so because…I endured…suffered…through those things with her.

Before I leave you, I would love for you to read my other book, "Change Him...In 100 Pages" It's the first book that teaches women how to change men. How to change a bad boy into a good man isn't the goal of every woman or the goal of this book. Teaching a good man how to handle a good this...is the goal of this book and hopefully...every woman. Go to www.ChangeAMan.com. Enjoy.

# About The Author

Devin T. Robinson X "Egypt" is an award winning actor, author of multiple relationship books and an activist for HIV education. He's traveled the world inspiring audiences to be accountable for what actions they control. From Amman, Jordan, Doha Qatar, Johannesburg South Africa, Trinidad, Tobago, Barbados and almost all of the United States, his message is borderless.

With two degrees, one in arts and the other in theatre, Egypt has used this knowledge to effectively translate the language of love in performance poetry infused with comedy, acting and motivational speaking. He dubs this unique form of education, "Confessional narration."

This God given talent has led him to a **TEDx** talk, World Famous Apollo Theatre,

BET's 106 & Park, MTV, National Public Radio in addition to many radio and newspaper interviews.

He donates all honor to his belief in God. With his future wife in tow, Egypt has turned a childhood filled with yesterday's pain into a "today" drowned in breathable love. He makes it a point to detail, without his sister, Chasity; he wouldn't be the man he is today. Egypt is proof that a woman can raise a man…but it's up to the man to be a man.

Read more, see videos and request Egypt at www.ChangeAMan.com or email YouCan@ChangeAMan.com

Stay in touch and be part of a long lasting love.

www.ingramcontent.com/pod-product-compliance
Lightning Source LLC
Chambersburg PA
CBHW032216040426
42449CB00005B/622